Be Fair!

Jennifer Overend Prior, Ph.D.

Consultants

Shelley Scudder
Gifted Education Teacher
Broward County Schools

Caryn Williams, M.S.Ed.
Madison County Schools
Huntsville, AL

Publishing Credits

Dona Herweck Rice, *Editor-in-Chief*
Lee Aucoin, *Creative Director*
Torrey Maloof, *Editor*
Diana Kenney, M.A.Ed., NBCT,
   Associate Education Editor
Marissa Rodriguez, *Designer*
Stephanie Reid, *Photo Editor*
Rachelle Cracchiolo, M.S.Ed., *Publisher*

Image Credits: Cover & pp. 1, 9 Alamy; back cover iStockphoto; pp. 19, 24 Corbis; p. 11 The Granger Collection; pp. 5, 7 iStockphoto; pp. 20, 21 (top) Shea Acosta; p. 15 The Library of Congress [LC-USZ62-131892]; p. 16 The Library of Congress [LC-USE6-D-008757]; p. 21 The Library of Congress [LC-USF33-005164-M5]; p. 10 Picture History/Newscom; p. 13 Beth Pachal; pp. 4, 6, 14, 17 ThinkStock; All other images from Shutterstock.

Teacher Created Materials

5301 Oceanus Drive
Huntington Beach, CA 92649-1030
http://www.tcmpub.com

ISBN 978-1-4333-6974-2
© 2014 Teacher Created Materials, Inc.

2

Table of Contents

Fair Is Fair

Try to be good and do all that you should. It is important to care. Do your part to be **fair**!

When you are fair, you treat people the same. You follow the rules. You give everyone an **equal** (EE-kwuhl) chance.

A boy and a girl share an ice cream cone.

These kids follow the rules in a card game.

Freedom

As a **citizen** (SIT-uh-zuhn) of the United States, you have **rights**. You have the right to go to school. You have the right to be treated fairly.

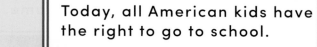

Today, all American kids have the right to go to school.

Bill of Rights

The Bill of Rights are laws that protect your **freedom**. Freedom is the power to do what you want to do.

Bill of Rights

You can **vote** to make a choice. You can vote on a game to play. You can vote on what food to eat. This is a fair way to choose things that are good for everyone. Grown-ups vote for our leaders. They make choices so we can have better lives.

This family votes on what to eat.

Vote for President

Grown-ups choose who will be president of the United States. The president is the leader of the country.

These grown-ups vote for president.

Do you know who Ben Franklin was? He worked for freedom. He wanted people to work together and be kind. He wanted people to live in peace. Ben was not afraid to speak out about being fair.

Ben Franklin

Busy Ben

Ben Franklin was a busy man. He was an inventor and a writer. He was a leader, too.

Ben helps write the Declaration of Independence.

Be Respectful

When you are fair, you treat others with **respect** (ri-SPEKT). Respect your parents and your teachers. Respect your friends. Listen, share, and do what they ask.

These students show respect for their teacher by raising their hands.

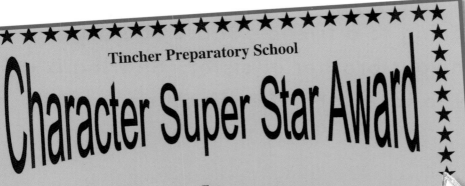

Tincher Preparatory School

Character Super Star Award

For

Justice and Fairness

Awarded to : _Jenna Pachal_ in Room _25_
For the Months of January/February.

Mr. Bill Vogel, Principal

Mr. David Echevarria, Counselor

This is an award a student won for being fair.

13

Sharing is fair. Share your time by listening to a friend. Share your toys with your brother or sister. Sharing is a way to take care of each other.

A girl shares her snack.

These kids from long ago share a drink.

Each person has the right to be heard. It is fair to take turns playing. It is also fair to take turns speaking. Look and listen when someone speaks. This is fair and shows respect.

Students take turns speaking in 1943.

Kids take turns speaking today.

The Golden Rule

The Golden Rule is very old. It says that you should treat others the way you want to be treated. When you follow this rule, you are being fair.

the Golden Rule

These friends are sharing a book.

Share It!

Is it fair to share? Are you being fair when you listen? Is it fair to take turns? Think of ways you can be fair. Draw pictures or write about your ideas. Share your ideas with your friends and family.

This girl writes a way she can be fair.

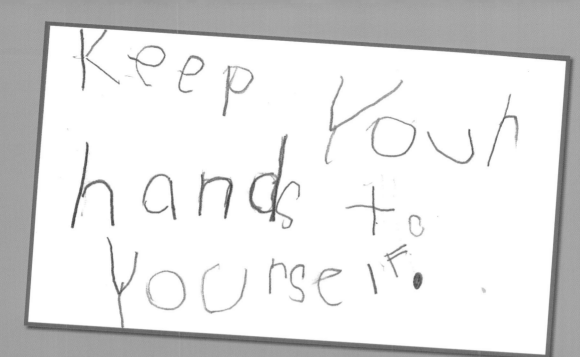

Keep Your hands to yourself.

These boys keep their hands to themselves.

Glossary

citizen—a person who lives in a country and has the rights of that country

equal—the same

fair—treating people the same

freedom—the power to do what you want to do

respect—the way you show that someone or something is important

rights—things people should be allowed to have, get, or do

vote—to make an official choice for or against someone or something

Index

Your Turn!

Be Nice!

The boys in the photo are being fair. They treat each other the way they want to be treated. That is the Golden Rule. Tell a friend about the Golden Rule. Talk about ways to be fair.